## From the section on grooming your neurotic dog:

Most dog owners are under the impression that dogs don't like baths. The major cause for this belief is that dogs hate baths. However, we must understand the underlying psychological reasons for dogs' aversion to soap and water. It occurs to most dogs that actually there is no need for them to get into a tub. They may smell bad to their owners, but this is a matter of opinion. To other dogs they smell just fine. In fact, a washed dog is often socially ostracized by its canine friends until it becomes its old self again. . . .

*Cartoons by*
## Eric Gurney

# How to Live with a Neurotic Dog

## by Stephen Baker

A KANGAROO BOOK
PUBLISHED BY POCKET BOOKS NEW YORK

# HOW TO LIVE WITH A NEUROTIC DOG

**Prentice-Hall edition published 1960**

**POCKET BOOK edition published November, 1976**
4th printing . . . June, 1977

This POCKET BOOK edition includes every word contained in
the original, higher-priced edition. It is printed from brand-new
plates made from completely reset, clear, easy-to-read type.
POCKET BOOK editions are published by
POCKET BOOKS,
a division of Simon & Schuster, Inc.,
A GULF + WESTERN COMPANY
Trademarks registered in the United States
and other countries.
In Canada distributed by PaperJacks Ltd.,
330 Steelcase Road, Markham, Ontario.

---

ISBN: 0-671-80788-9.

4587

*To Bobo—a dachshund—one of the most outstanding neurotic personalities of our time*

# Contents

# How to Live with a Neurotic Dog

# 1

# What Makes a Dog Neurotic?

We must, first of all, try to understand the neurotic dog. Our understanding is the key to his happiness, if not our own.

There is a reason for everything a dog does. In his opinion, these reasons are valid, whether we humans think so or not. If, for example, he takes the breast of fried chicken from the dining room table before we are able to eat it, there is a reason for that. A very good reason. He's hungry.

**A great many dogs are neurotic, especially in this country.** The canine population of the United States is about 25 million. Out of this, about 25 million can be classified as neurotic—a conservative estimate.

As a matter of fact, psychiatrists agree that neurosis among dogs is on the increase. More and more, dog owners are asking for psychiatric treatment.

Today's dog lives under more pressure than ever before in history. His schedule is demanding; chores confront him every minute of the day. The heavy strain put on the modern dog causes many to crack up.

Here is a typical schedule of the average dog of today.

| | |
|---|---|
| 7:30-7:55 | Thinks about getting up. |
| 7:55-8:00 | Jumps off bed; shakes thoroughly. Ambles to kitchen where there seems to be some activity. |
| 8:00-8:15 | Participates at the breakfast table. |
| 8:15-10:00 | Walks back to the bedroom. Sleeps. |
| 10:00-11:30 | Accompanies mistress of the house as she shops. At the supermarket, lifts a bag of peanuts from the lowest shelf. Chase. Eats on the run. Loses mistress and has to walk home. |
| 11:30-12:00 | Before-meal nap in bedroom. |
| 12:00-12:45 | Adjourns to living room sofa. Continuation of nap. |
| 12:45-1:30 | Chased off sofa. Back to bedroom in search of privacy. Nap. |
| 1:30-2:30 | Ejected from bedroom. Removed from sofa. Walks down to basement. Nap. |
| 2:30-2:50 | Greets children returning from school. Jumps up and down, wags tail, licks faces, etc., to make good impression. |

| | |
|---|---|
| 2:50-2:51 | Eats meal of dog food. |
| 2:51-3:15 | Participates at meal with children and their mother. |
| 3:15-3:30 | After-meal nap. |
| 3:30-4:00 | Calls on neighbor, a dachshund named Mozart. Joins rest of gang in search of female companionship. Visits Julie, a Pekingese, but finds she is locked up in the house for some reason. Too bad. |
| 4:00-4:15 | Fights with the boys. |
| 4:15-4:16 | Takes short cut across the Taylors' garden. |
| 4:16-4:30 | Pursued by Mrs. Taylor. Boys disperse. |
| 4:30-4:35 | Leaps into stream to lose Mrs. Taylor. She can't swim. |
| 4:35-4:45 | Enters living room. Lifted up by back of neck and put out the back door with orders to dry off. |
| 4:45-5:30 | Nap in garage. |
| 5:30-6:30 | Helps mistress of house get dinner ready. |
| 6:30-7:30 | Participates at family dinner. |
| 7:30-7:55 | Watches television, an adult Western. Naps through second half of program. |
| 7:55-8:00 | Awakened by shooting on television. Badman falls off horse. He's dead. Continues nap. |
| 8:00-8:01 | Walks to bedroom. |
| 8:01 | Retires. |

We should remember that the little puppy, when he first enters the world, has no emotional problems. *As in the case of the human infant, problems come later in life, possibly a few seconds after birth.*

One of the foremost thoughts which occurs to a newborn dog and which strikes him as a brilliant idea

is EAT. Right away, conflict sets in. Instinct pushes him toward satisfying his hunger, but environmental factors may stop him. Such factors consist of his small but equally determined brothers and sisters, all with the very same idea; his path to the source of milk may be blocked by the rest of the family. At once, frustration sets in. For the rest of his life he may remember the incident and develop a nervous complex at the thought of food.

A dog's life is becoming increasingly competitive. There are more dogs around than ever before. Everywhere the dog looks, he meets the eyes of other dogs. There are stores where dogs can be had for a price; often as many as half a dozen dogs are placed in a show window, and passersby are apt to praise them vocally in the presence of dogs who also happen to be passing by. *It comes as a shock to even the most self-confident dog that he can be replaced.*

Reminding the dog of his inadequacy are his contemporaries who, through practically no effort of their own, manage to make their mark in the world.

Even in his own home, away from the dog race (canine equivalent of "rat race"), the dog is reminded of his own shortcomings by references to others who are making canine history.

A dog named Laika, for instance, became an international celebrity overnight (despite her Russian citizenship) when she was sent into orbit. Actually, Laika did only what any other dog would have done in her place. It would have been foolhardy of her to desert the rocket en route.

Snoopy, a dog who gained fame through frequent appearances in the comics, is often admired for his sense of humor and his ability to think aloud. Hundreds send letters to him which are opened by Charles Schulz, the only one who knows that Snoopy really does not exist.

There can be no doubt about Lassie's existence, on the other hand. Everybody loves this remarkable collie, except other dogs. A top television performer, Lassie makes a specialty of swimming across swift mountain streams: for this he gets paid. Lassie's relationship to his owner is ideal—he supports his master.

I SUPPORT
MY MASTER

Dogs of uncertain pedigree are often made to feel socially inferior. Pure ancestry assures entrée to dog shows, while doors are closed to the most numerous and perhaps most successful breed of all: the mutt.

Our culture makes severe demands on the dog. We humans just accept, on hearsay, the premise that "dog is man's best friend" and act accordingly. This is a debatable issue for the dog himself, however, and we can hardly blame him. He knows that, if anything, the reverse is true—man is dog's best friend and as such has certain responsibilities toward his pet.

Unless the dog grows up to be a Saint Bernard or a Great Dane, which not all dogs can do, he will be at the mercy of his master. Man is bigger than his dog. Most of the time he walks on two legs, not four, which makes him appear even taller. Worse still, man's vertical position enables him to look *down* at his pet. This height gives him an illusion of superiority, a state of mind of which he rarely lets go.

*Even to a puppy it soon becomes obvious that his chief obstacle in life is, and always will be, his master.* Locomoting on his legs, man has his hands free to do other things. If the dog is average in stature, and most dogs are, man will easily be able to grasp him by the scruff of his neck, lift him, and deposit him wherever it seems most practical under the circumstances.

A dog's instinct, coupled with common sense, tells him that feeding time is all day. Man insists on giving him only one or two meals, however, instead of a hundred. The food he gets is inferior. In typically human fashion, dog owners cling to the notion that their pets demand a special kind of nourishment. This is not true. Dog's needs are the same as human's; roast turkey will do.

Dog's natural habitat is on top of the bed, preferably a freshly made bed. His acute sense of self-preservation tells him this is where he belongs. But his master, ignorant of the emotional needs of his dog, may interrupt his pet's daily 24-hour nap and insist that he stay on the floor, which, as even people know, is not as soft as the bed. Or, the owner may even require his dog to go outdoors for periods of time and expose himself to wind, sun, and rain.

*Dog learns early in life to depend on his intellect rather than his size.* He realistically accepts the fact that nature made man a larger, more powerful creature who excels at jumping and in climbing trees. But he knows that physical prowess puts his master at only a temporary advantage, and that in

the long run dog's superior reasoning power will win out. Dog has the ability to wait patiently for his turn. He plans his moves way ahead. At times, he lets man feel he is his intellectual equal to throw him off balance.

And so, quietly but with remarkable efficiency, he fights his battle against man. In the process he often becomes neurotic. So does his master.

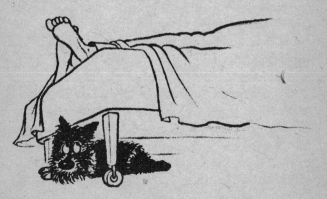

IS IT ANY WONDER DOGS
GET NEUROTIC?
THEY HAVE LOST THEIR ABILITY
TO RELAX!

## *Summary of Chapter 1*

1. DO be patient with your neurotic dog. Try to understand the underlying cause of his neurosis: it's you.

2. DON'T praise other dogs in his presence. It may make him feel insignificant.

3. DO consider his deep-seated instincts, such as hunger and sleepiness.

4. DON'T make your mutt feel socially inferior. Tell him in this country it's not who you are but what you are.

5. DO remember: Dog's Best Friend Is His Master. This means you.

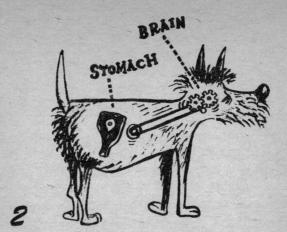

# 2
# *Training the Neurotic Dog*

It isn't too difficult to train a neurotic dog, providing we use psychology instead of common sense.

His education should start at an early age. It may take the dog a lifetime to learn. The adage "You can't teach an old dog new tricks" has no validity. You can't teach new tricks to a young dog either.

This does not mean he is stupid. Man often fails to get through to his dog simply because of the language barrier. His dog just does not understand him. Few people achieve proficiency in barking, and when they do their performance only tends to confuse their listeners.

It has yet to be proved to a dog that his readiness to obey will actually improve his lot. Cats, for example, hardly ever pay attention to a command, yet they have man's respect. Birds and fish do even less for a living, yet they get fed as often as the dog does.

Nevertheless, dogs have been known to comply with their masters' wishes, for beneath it all dogs are anxious to please. Dogs are affectionate by nature and believe firmly that they, too, should be included in the brotherhood of man. In the world of dogdom there is no room for hate; given a choice, for example, they will prefer a pat on the head to a kick in the rear.

Love and tenderness will go a long way toward bringing about a change in the neurotic dog without emotionally upsetting him. A case in point is a young poodle who once lived in an apartment. Like any dog in the first ten years or so of its life, he was fond of chewing up books, with a special preference for those on the lower shelves of the bookcase. Aware of the tenets of modern psychology, the master did not waste his time admonishing his growing dog, but went straight to the core of the problem. He built another bookcase with shelves out of the dog's reach. As the dog grew larger, he built another; some years later he took his few remaining volumes to the attic. His dog gave up the chewing habit completely. The master gave up reading.

Every dog can be taught to do tricks if properly approached, no matter how neurotic he or his master happens to be.

**Fundamentally, teaching a dog means developing his reflexes.** As everyone knows from Pavlov's experiments, a dog will learn to react to the same sounds and gestures automatically if repeated often enough. Here's the way this works:

Let's say you would like to make your pet learn the command STAY. Every time you want him to stay, you scream STAY and also hold up your hand to remind him that both your voice and hand signal mean he must not move. Slowly you back away from him, still holding up your hand. You keep walking, increasing the distance between you. If you trip over something, never mind. Get up and keep walking, remembering to hold your hand in position.

Now that your dog has obeyed your command, release him from his position and ask him to come to you. Be sure to praise him when he reaches your side. A bone or two will go a long way in assuring him of your satisfaction. In fact, you might keep a variety of foods on hand for a reward.

Soon you won't have to use the command "stay" at all. Your dog will instinctively know what your raised hand has come to mean. Every time you show your dog the palm of your hand, signaling him to "stay," he will get up—even from the deepest of slumber—and walk right up to you, insisting it is feeding time.

---

Dogs, like human infants, learn best by imitation. Show him what you want, and he may respond to your efforts by performing. In any case, he will be entertained.

EVERY DOG SHOULD UNDERSTAND BASIC COMMANDS, SUCH AS "NO," "SIT," "HEEL," "DOWN," "COME," AND "HEY! NOT ON THE CARPET." THE FOLLOWING PAGES CONTAIN HELPFUL SUGGESTIONS FOR TRAINING YOUR NEUROTIC DOG.

NO — O — O — OO — O

# 1. THE "NO" COMMAND

One of the most important words in your dog's vocabulary is NO. He must learn that NO is the antonym of YES, even though the two words sound so similar to him as to cause confusion.

The word NO must be used judiciously. A sharp NO may carry with it the implication that the dog is not wanted. One of the ways of softening your NO is to deliver it in a series, as in NO, NO, NO. The emphasis is on the last NO. As a further modification of the common NO, NO, NO, some folks, when displeased, say NO, NO, NO, *NO*. This procedure proves prudent in cases where you are dealing with a weary animal; four NO's keep him awake longer than three.

An excellent version of the peremptory NO command is one popular with women dog lovers. It goes something like this: "No-o-o . . . No-o-o . . . Sha-a-a-me on you." The first No-o-o may be emitted in a low pitch, then worked gradually to a high pitch, until the voice cracks. Or it may be delivered the other way round. To the average neurotic dog, both versions sound not too unpleasant (they remind him of his mother), and neither will hurt his feelings.

A few dog owners have developed the habit of spelling out the word NO to their dogs; i.e., "NO! Do you hear? N . . . O." This is unnecessary. NO is an exceptionally easy word to spell; the implication that the listener is not erudite enough to comprehend such an elementary word is an insult.

## 2. MAKING YOUR DOG "SIT"

Every dog should know how to sit. He should not lie sleeping all of the time.

*The first problem to be overcome in teaching your neurotic dog to sit* down *is to make him stand* up. Hit him gently on the flank. If this fails to rouse him, strike again, this time with more force. If he still does not respond (as he probably won't), try smelling salts.

Once you have succeeded in making your dog stand up, you are halfway through the job. It is relatively simple to make a standing dog sit down, since the tendency is to go back to the original supine position and, in the process, he must go through the motions of sitting down. Your problem is to catch him in time, before he is prone on the ground again.

This can be done by taking a firm grip on the scruff of his neck or, better yet, by pulling up on the leash. The purpose here is to keep his head *up* at a safe distance from the ground. Let his backside sink down while you are holding his head up. You

**STEP ONE**

**STEP TWO**

**STEP THREE**

**STEP FOUR**

**STEP FIVE**

will find that your dog is now in a natural sitting position.

This pose he will maintain as long as you are able to keep his head up. Once you slacken your grip, the dog will, of course, fall to the ground and resume the prone position.

## 3. TRAINING THE DOG TO "HEEL"

There are times in every dog's life when he must be taken for a walk, especially when his home is an apartment several stories above the street so that putting him out the window or door becomes a somewhat unsatisfactory solution—to the dog, at least.

*To take a pet for a walk requires a leash and a collar. The idea is that these implements will prevent the dog from carrying out his natural desire to run away.*

First, put your dog on your left side and then hold on to the leash. Don't give the dog too much leeway. If he rushes ahead, run after him. If he stops, you stop. Expect stopovers at every fire hydrant (no matter how often passed), tree, other dog, and puddle on the street that may strike him, if not you, as interesting. If he wants to cross the street, don't let him get too far from you. See if you can make it to the other side without upsetting drivers.

It is vital that your pet learn to stay close to your left knee. This position is not too hard to maintain. If the dog crosses in front of you, simply about-face and walk the other way. If the dog circles around

you, keep rotating with him as fast as you can, or you will find that the leash has tied up your legs so that neither of you can walk. If you become hopelessly entangled, ask a passerby (who has probably stopped to watch) to unwind you. But, under no circumstances should you permit your dog to walk on your right side. Always keep to *his* right.

### 4. TEACHING THE "DOWN" COMMAND

Not much effort is needed to make the neurotic dog fully understand—and approve of—the command DOWN. As pointed out earlier, the chief problem is to convey the importance of the command UP.

### 5. GIVING THE "COME" LESSON TO YOUR DOG

To teach the dog to COME, you will need the collar again, a length of cord (about 50 feet or so), and the dog himself.

Get the collar on the pet, tie one end of the cord to the collar, and hold on to the other end. Let the dog get away from you about 10 or 15 feet. If he won't wake up, or he just won't go away, *you* walk away. Then say, "Come here."

If there is no reaction, try "Please come here," or, perhaps, "Will you be good enough to come here, please?"

If these requests aren't responded to, give the cord a gentle jerk. *If still nothing happens, pull again, this time with more authority.* Then once more. Now get up from the floor and replace the broken cord.

Soon you will have developed much muscle power through weeks of concentrated training in pulling the dog toward you while he maintains his original DOWN position.

Once you find you can drag him as much as 10 or 15 feet, you may begin work on the advanced version of the COME command. This merely involves increasing the distances between you to 20 feet or more.

Sometimes, a distance of 50 feet will give your dog a chance to get out of sight by hiding behind a bush. Don't be frightened. You will always be able to find him. Just follow the cord.

## 6. HOUSEBREAKING

A dog who is not housebroken is a great inconvenience to his owner. For this reason, most dog owners insist that their pets learn the difference between table legs and fire hydrants, no matter how similar they may appear to be.

The toilet training received by the neurotic dog in early life is extremely significant from a psychological point of view. Confused concepts result later in serious emotional disturbances in the mental health of the owner.

You should be neither too lenient nor too harsh with the puppy. Overindulgence may mean that he will use the living room as a bathroom. Too much discipline, on the other hand, may mean that in his effort not to displease you, he will never again perform his natural functions *anywhere* under *any* circumstances.

Training your dog to use the outdoors is really not too complicated. Training should start with a constant vigil lasting four or five days and nights. It is best to start the lessons at the beginning of a two weeks' vacation so that you may devote the proper time to the welfare of your dog.

Diligent supervision will enable you to catch your pupil just in time. Alerted, you then say "No!" perhaps adding a few other words. Open the door and heave. After a week or so, catch up on your sleep.

In instances where the outdoors cannot be reached in time, the newspaper technique may be more practical. Spread several thicknesses on the floor (after you have read them). For small dogs, three to five layers; for medium-sized dogs, seven to ten; for large breeds, a couple of magazines.

Place the puppy on the newspaper every two hours. Soon he will perform as regularly as Old Faithful. When he has learned the purpose of a newspaper, he may go out of his way to find one. At this time, caution must be exercised about leaving newspapers on living room sofas.

It should be remembered that today's canine has the same dislike of slovenly homes as a human. *The neurotic dog's instinctive preference for clean living quarters shows itself in the well-known habit of covering up his marks by kicking dirt over them, even though this might mean digging a hole in the living room carpet.*

41

... transit facilities,
...portation program may
...st hope for improving

...nergetic public servant
...contributions. We agree
...wayway program be
...th of 66th Street, and
...ut on the question of
...ongested midtown and
...laid down by the City
...e upheld.

## ...rth Control

...nt that Pope Paul VI
... opinion of his special
...h control and also that
...in the recent encyclical
... incorrectly interpreted
... present doctrine.
...shops' report since
...as issued several
...tional Roman
...thods of birth
...ished within
...ore Roman
...d his mind,
...il does not
...such a great
...However, his
...t. Change, in the
...ctice without the
...its prohibition.
...priest, whether
...istr of the most
...ons of Roman
...sing contraception
...rting to abortion
...h has survived for
...y factors. One
...d accept the fact
...Today's reality
...is a necessity.

## ...the Freeze

...nt plans to extend its
...wages and prices when
...July. The hope is that
...ial leaders will exercise
...ne Minister Wilson does
...n defenses against infla-
...ses. So the Government
...spend any increases that
...n's competitive position.

...ns are of course opposed
...freedom of action. But
...ces and wages in excess
...a some form of control.
...improved Britain's bal-
...i strengthened the pound
...program, which features
...ot yet produced a more

---

### The Missin...

By C. L. ...

CASTEAU...
position...
lantic...
that...
gan...
to...

... action

...r Alone
...e Gaulle
...insistence
...not automatic
...any war in t
...ance will de
...is an o
...ther the mea
...of the North
...rom General
...point, this ma
...to plan for th
...with Consequently.

---

### ...he Editor of T...

## Support C...
## Gun-Cont...

To the Editor:

I am a few days late in writing to express my appreciation for the editorial in your issue of

It is advisable to read the newspaper *before*.

every American, and I join with you in your hope that Congress will enact gun-control legislation this year even in the face of the powerful lobby mentioned in your editorial.

We experienced in New Jersey something in the nature of the ordeal presently facing the

... at least should
...bow to the state.
"At Nuremberg we hanged "patriotic" Germans who claimed that the state's moral authority transcended their own. In a recent trial for murdering a Viet...an
...ki, by
...the
civilian. In convicting him, the court-martial board asserted that he should have refused to obey such an order.
Indeed, the Geneva convention maintains that private soldiers need not obey orders from superior officers which will entail crimes against humanity.

time political
man. Student
Responsible Cit
1966), I have l
entering an en
sional communi
I would expect
major spokesm
munity, to rep
the news in h
you have show
million respon
guished citizen
end to the po
bankruptcy of

R...
New Yo...

N... Ci...

The question is often asked: is housebreaking really worth the effort? Does the result justify the tremendous outlay of energy spent in teaching a dog? The only possible answer is an enthusiastic YES. Besides, is there a choice? You cannot live with a dog who is not housebroken. You must move out.

Some dogs don't want to learn. They oppose the principle of the whole idea; they do not accept their master as an authoritative figure and cannot agree that he is smarter than they are.

In such cases it is recommended to get outside, professional help. Today there are special classes held for slow learners, dogs and people. The faculty consists of experts well versed in canine psychology; usually at hand are a wild animal tamer, who snaps instructions at dogs and their owners, and his assistant, who carries a small broom and a dirt pan and closes up the line of dogs.

At first dogs may be reluctant to participate in such organized group activities; they are usually bored by the proceedings. But once inside. . . .

they become exemplary students. What a gratifying
sight it is to watch an obedience class at work! Dogs
who had never even given their masters as much as
an answer have now become mild and well-behaved

personalities, eager to improve themselves. Day after
day they attend the sessions, always adding to their
knowledge, until . . .

graduation time. This is the day they have all been waiting for. Was it worth all the effort, the toil that went into learning? Of course it was.

# *Summary of Chapter 2*

1. DO make sure your dog understands you. Learn to pronounce words correctly.

2. DON'T try to communicate with your dog in his own language, even though it might be simpler for you than speaking English. Most humans cannot learn to bark properly.

3. DO explain his mistakes to him. All dogs prefer persuasion to force, especially when the latter is directed against them.

4. DON'T push your dog around. He may bite you. If he does, chide him and call an ambulance.

5. DO remember: kindness goes a long way. One happy dog is worth 100 unhappy masters.

# 3
# Sleeping Habits of
# the Neurotic Dog

Dog's most essential activity in life is sleeping. He needs sleep to recuperate, to summon sufficient energy to get up, to eat several times a day. The average neurotic dog may require approximately 24 hours of rest a day.

Occasionally one hears of a case where a dog owner kept his pet awake for several consecutive hours. Dogs should not be asked to perform such feats. Keeping his eyes open for such intervals may seriously impair the dog's emotional health; he gets bored. Soon he will have a total nervous collapse; probably on top of your bed.

Those who truly care for their pets see that they are made comfortable. In the living room this may

Sling chairs are not designed for dogs or humans.

Side chairs are too small to support the average dog.

Coffee tables have tops that are too hard.

not be so easy since most contemporary furniture has not been primarily designed to accommodate dogs. *Today's chairs are all right for humans to sit on, but most dogs prefer lying down on them; tables are often built with a flagrant disregard for the natural contours of the dog's body.*

*The single piece of furniture which seems to answer most completely dog's eternal search for suitable sleeping quarters is the Bed.*

To a dog, the Bed is an amazing invention, perhaps the most perfect, and certainly the most useful ever devised by humans.

The top of the bed allows the dog to stretch out in any direction he wishes. He can shift his position freely; in the daytime he can find the sunniest spot. If the temperature is below the required level, it is possible to throw the bedspread on the floor and get under the blanket. The sheets are clean, unlike the carpet where humans thoughtlessly tread day after day with their shoes on or, worse yet, in the evening with their shoes off. There are usually pillows on the bed, light enough to carry away to needed locations.

Through most of the day the dog is able to find privacy in the bedroom; he can sleep undisturbed. In the kitchen he may be stepped on, or he may step on someone's feet; in the living room he may be sat on, while reclining on the couch. But in the bedroom he is about as far away as he can hope to get from those with whom he must share the home.

*As a piece of furniture, the bed has only a single disadvantage to dogs: man, too, thinks that is where he should sleep.* Dogs often find their midday siesta rudely interrupted at eleven or so at

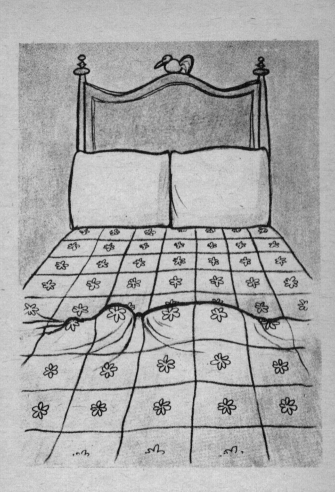

night when the master makes an appearance in pajamas, and insists on sharing quarters. A struggle then begins which sometimes lasts far into the night, occasionally till morning.

Although no dog *likes* to share a bed with humans, there are ways in which a dog can improve the situation. A few examples will be given here:

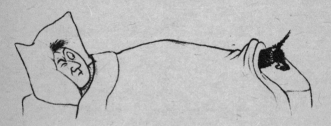

The burrower knows that the warmest spot is **under the blanket**. Working his way through the maze of folds, he usually arrives safely at his favorite place.

The digger needs a hollow to sleep in, probably for protection against mythical enemies. He tries to scoop out a hole on top of the blankets, and sometimes he succeeds.

The snuggler keeps close, close to his human partner. His devotion is flattering to man; it has practical value to the dog, who knows men make excellent hot water bottles.

The sleepwalker makes brief journeys at night to the kitchen (for a midnight snack) or outdoors (for a variety of reasons). This type, driven by a sense of urgency, often takes shortcuts.

The pillow sharer does not believe that a pillow should serve **only** as a headrest. Perhaps for man, yes, but not for dog.

The jumper goes joyfully to bed. The bed is soft enough to absorb his landing, and so is his master.

The early riser wakes with the sun, welcomes the day with a burst of enthusiasm. He likes to share these feelings with his master; having done so, he goes back to sleep.

The large dog would **like** to share the bed with his master. Unfortunately, because of the size of the bed, this is not always possible.

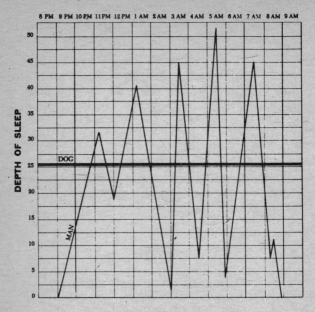

**SLEEPING CHART OF DOGS**

As far as the dog is concerned, men make strange bedfellows, indeed. Tossing and turning, men go to sleep and wake up in the morning more tired than ever. During the night they mumble words even more incomprehensible than those uttered in their wakeful moments.

In contrast to man's nocturnal habits are those of dog. Sleep chart above shows how the average dog sleeps through the night.

*Some dog owners refuse to share their beds with pets.* For these people, the following step-by-

**step** procedure of how to get a dog off the bed may be helpful.

First, get the dog within reach of your hands. Start out with gentle persuasion. If this fails to have any effect, and it always does, begin the use of legs and body. Undulating movements of the torso may roll the dog toward you so you can grab him. Push forcefully now, using your hands. If he bites, tear off part of the sheet for a bandage.

If your dog is under the blanket (and most smarter breeds prefer this location) do not grope for him blindly. The wisest course is to lift up the blanket gradually. This is best achieved by getting out of bed. Do not yank the blanket off quickly since sudden movements will annoy the dog and he will fight for what he thinks belongs to him.

Studies of dogs' twitching tails and quivering
noses indicate beyond doubt that they experi-

ence vivid dreams. Shown here are the nocturnal fantasies of a female dog.

It is entirely possible that the dog will remain asleep even after you have taken the cover off. Try the pillow method. If the pillow bursts, do not despair, you can always buy a new one. Then jump up and down on the mattress for a few minutes.

At this point some dogs (those known as "watch dogs") will slowly open one or both eyes, although they will probably not be willing to leave the bed. Your next move is to rock the bed. Lift one end of the bed, then drop it firmly on the floor. Pull off the mattress. Turn the whole bed over.

If all of these efforts come to nothing, let him know that you mean business. Impress on the dog that you're the sort of fellow who sticks with his convictions; you will *not* share your bed with him. Get another blanket from the linen closet and go to sleep on the living room sofa.

---

A well-known method of keeping dogs off their masters' beds (approved by the Society for the Prevention of Cruelty to Animals and also by dogs themselves) is to build a bed for canine use only.

To make the contrivance acceptable to a dog, it must have features all its own.

Dish next to bed (1) provides nourishment to dozing dog. Slight movement of dog's head allows him to quench his thirst (2). Innerspring mattress, not too soft (3), follows contours of dog's body (see insert). Stairs leading to bed (4) save him from having to jump up. Frame of bed is mahogany (5) to give this piece of furniture an authentic look. Pillows (6) may be used either for resting or chewing. To lull the dog to sleep is a music box (7). Picture of sweetheart (8) helps dog have pleasant dreams. Large rotating fan (9) circulates stuffy air without disturbing dog's sleep.

# *Summary of Chapter 3*

1. DO remember a dog needs sleep when he is tired, which is at all times. His is not an easy existence; he lives a dog's life.

2. DON'T disturb him while he is getting his rest. Speak only in a whisper and walk on tiptoe. Don't worry about burglars. They will do just that anyway.

3. DO get a comfortable bed for yourself. Your pet will appreciate your thoughtfulness when he moves in with you.

4. DON'T let him interrupt your night's sleep, however. If he wakes you up often, try sleeping pills.

5. DO try an electric blanket for cold nights. Dogs like warmth.

6. DON'T—*please*—snore.

# 4

# How to Dress and Groom the Neurotic Dog

For centuries dogs ran around naked. Modern civilization put an end to that. Today, thanks to man's thoughtfulness, there is clothing to fit every dog, no matter what the dog's girth, height, or budget.

It is important to outfit your dog properly. Contrary to popular belief, dogs *like* to be dressed up—especially if they are neurotic. Clothing gives the dog a sense of importance, a sense of equality with his master. If his attire is more elegant than the master's (as is often the case), it makes him feel even more equal.

There are practical aspects to being properly attired. In the winter, clothing keeps the dog warm; in the summer it keeps him positively hot. Clothing

keeps the dog cleaner; to wash his clothes is less trouble than to wash the dog.

Most important, the kind of clothes the dog wears enables other dogs to tell at a glance whether the wearer is male or female, eliminating the effort of crossing the street for a routine check.

*Dogs often dress for each other. They learn quickly that clothes are status symbols.* Clothes can make them look rich or poor, sophisticated or hillbilly.

Dogs may keep their feelings bottled up, but inwardly they fret if they pass a better-dressed dog on the street. It is often the costume that makes a dog stand out from others who may look disturbingly like him when undressed.

Clothes should fit the dog's personality. Today's dog owner is in the position of being able to choose wisely from a variety of outfits so that the dog's hidden personality may emerge.

Clothes are especially important to the female dog. She thinks a great deal about her appearance.

Feminine fashions change rapidly. Waistlines move from bust to buttock and back again, hemlines shoot up and down. It pays to keep up with the trends by checking through magazines of fashion. There is nothing so disheartening to a female dog as having *nothing to wear*.

Most dog owners are under the impression that dogs don't like baths. The major cause for this belief is that dogs hate baths.

However, we must understand the underlying psychological reasons for dogs' aversion to soap and water. It occurs to most dogs that actually there is

Trenchcoat look is favored by dogs suspicious by profession, such as watch dogs.

Ladies' man is perhaps the most clothes-conscious of all dogs. He knows clothes make the dog.

Gray flannel suit, three-buttoned, narrow-shouldered, is for the young cosmopolitan.

The suburbanite likes casual garb to go with his easy, outdoor life.

Collegiate type takes pride in his heavy woolen sweater displaying a large letter in front. He is the athletic type.

Dignified dog appeals to other dogs with his air of mystery.

Dress gathered around the waist with large ribbon is designed to follow dog's figure, more or less. Slit in back allows tail to move about freely.

Flamboyant straw hat for summer wear is popular with females who like to keep up appearances even on hot days.

Peaked fur cap, for wintry days, falls gently about the shoulders. This headpiece helps point up the dog's most distinctive feature, her nose.

A variety of shoes is available for delicate feet. Heavy rubber boots (left) prevent any moisture from seeping through while the dog goes out for a short walk. Woolen socks (right) are for indoor use, will keep the dog's feet clean.

Female dogs like brief bathing suits. They may not go into the water, but on land they will make an impression.

Male swimming trunks show off a fine athletic body.

For those who don't care.

no need for him to get into a tub. He may smell bad to his owner, but this is a matter of opinion. To other dogs he smells just fine. In fact, a washed dog is often socially ostracized by his canine friends until he becomes his old self again.

Bathing a dog requires patience, understanding, and brute strength. The step-by-step procedure shown here may be helpful to owners who want their dogs not only clean—but happy, too.

**1**

Explain to your dog why you think he should be clean. Tell him, nice dogs are clean dogs.

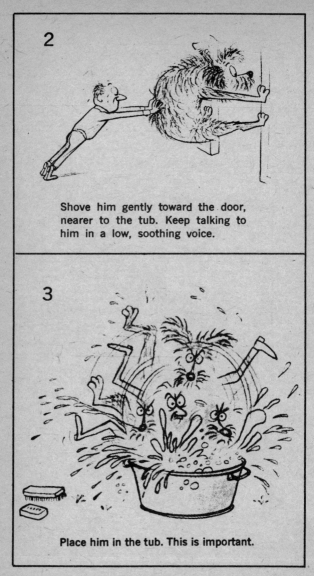

**2**

Shove him gently toward the door, nearer to the tub. Keep talking to him in a low, soothing voice.

**3**

Place him in the tub. This is important.

**4**

Now get out of the tub.

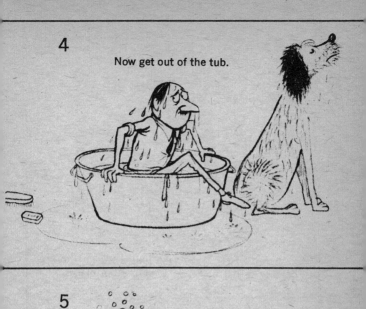

**5**

With brush in one hand, soap in the other, start washing him.

**6**

Wash him thoroughly, even at hard-to-get-at places.

**7**

Let him shake himself. Remember: a dry dog is better than a wet dog.

**8**

Refreshed by the bath, dog will want to work off pent-up energy. Encourage him to roam around the house a bit.

**9**

Now rest.

Being well-groomed increases a dog's feelings of self-esteem. Today, there is a variety of canine hair-dos (you can see similar ones on human heads). Even male dogs find they can do something with their hair.

Crew cut is primarily for the younger set. Hair will stand straight up if cut properly.

Bearded look for males gives an intellectual mien. Female dogs, especially those from the big city, seem to find this look irresistible.

Natural look enjoys great popularity with dogs proud of being dogs. Its greatest advantage is the fact that it requires no combing.

Wigs can be bought today for the female dog with a flair for the unusual. The possibilities are as limitless as the imagination of the dog.

A well-groomed dog is a happy dog.

# Summary of Chapter 4

1. DON'T embarrass your dog by making him go out with no clothes on.

2. DO consider his personal preferences when choosing outfits.

3. DON'T dress your dog in last year's fashion.

4. DO leave an opening in the back for his tail, etc.

5. DON'T forget: a dress may be worn with or without a belt.

6. DO use plenty of soap and water. After an arduous workout, your dog will welcome the idea of a bath. Go ahead and take one.

**Roomiest traveling area** is, naturally, the back seat. It is ideally suited to the emotional needs of the traveling dog.

# 5

# Traveling with the Neurotic Dog

Dogs approve of traveling. It gives them a sense of getting away from it all—their environment, their masters. Weary of the routine which humans impose on them, the average neurotic dogs of today find no other outlet for their energy at home than to plunk down on the nearest soft chair and go to sleep. Welcome, indeed, is the sight of new places, such as the top of a hotel bed.

Dogs enjoy a change of scene so much that they cheerfully put up with hardships concomitant with travel. Moving from one place to another, a feat without which traveling is not possible, may call for sustained periods of activity. Cases are known where dogs have been made to walk several blocks from hotel to railroad station. Rarely, however, do the dogs complain.

As a rule, dogs think well of the means of transportation devised by men except, possibly, for the dog-sled. It makes little difference to them whether they are asked to travel by air, sea, or ground; any mechanical contrivance that conveys one physically from one place to another plays—in the dog's opinion—an important part in civilized existence.

The automobile, however, makes considerable demands on the dog's nervous system. Shown below are suggestions for how his trip can be made more comfortable when traveling by car.

**Good driving habits** will permit your dog to catch up on his sleep. Turns should be made carefully; five to ten miles an hour will be suitable. Avoid screeching of tires.

**Come to a stop gradually.** Sudden stops will jar the dog; even if he doesn't wake up, the jolt may cause him to have a bad dream.

Today's dogs have made remarkable adjustments to the ordeal of traveling by automobile. Wise owners have learned not to interfere with the dog's enjoyment of the trip; they let him be himself—a dog.

***Always remember: it was your idea to take this trip, not his.***

The sightseer likes to keep his eye on the scenery so he can check on passing cars and sneer at dogs being taken on a forced march. For clear visibility in the car, the dog will need the windows down summer or winter.

The lap dog demonstrates his affection by assuming a position in the driver's lap. Here he will steadfastly remain with typical canine devotion.

The joiner wants to make friends with everyone.

Travel lover can't wait to get into the car.

The recluse has an instinct for seeking dark corners in the car where he can catch up on his sleep.

The rear guard watches the world go by through his picture window. Much can be seen without having to lift or rotate head; rolling of eyeballs is the only physical effort needed here.

86

For reasons that are probably clear to them alone, most dogs consider the insides of automobiles their private domain and will take stern measures to protect this area against intruders. Filling station attendants come under the heading of intruders. This presents something of a problem when the driver finds himself in need of gas.

To forestall close bodily contact between dog and gas station attendant, some drivers keep their windows closed throughout the transaction. Communication may be a little tricky under these circumstances, but not impossible.

Yell instructions from inside the car.

Use hand signals to indicate number of gallons wanted.

Roll **windows down slightly** to provide some contact with the man on the other side.

If nothing else works, **take a calculated risk.** Open the window completely.

Railroads and airlines usually request owners to keep their pets in some kind of container. Traveling cases for this purpose can be purchased or made at home. The best cases are those with plenty of air-holes, allowing the dog to breathe freely or, if he feels this has become necessary, take a peek outside.

Large dogs require large traveling cases.

Dogs like to yelp, whine, and in other ways talk to themselves en route. As fellow passengers may think the sounds come from the owner himself, soundproofing cases may save considerable embarrassment.

Dog owners, planning their vacations, often ask: What kind of vacation is best for my pet? Where would he be his happiest, most relaxed self?

The answer should not be as difficult as some people imagine. Actually, the needs of dogs are simple and basic. Food is one of them; a hotel that will serve a steak too rare or too well done won't do, for example. Dogs approve of the custom of having their masters' breakfast served in bed. Also, dogs prefer to relax on well-made beds during the day, so the maid service might be given some thought before choosing a hotel.

Organized social activity, part of many a vacation routine, is looked upon with dismay by the majority of canines. By a wonder of nature, dogs are able to organize their day with sure instinct, requiring no outside help in order to sleep through the day without interruption.

*Perhaps the greatest dilemma dog owners find themselves in is this: Are mountain resorts preferable to seashore places?*

As a rule dogs prefer the latter. Their choice is based on logic. Mountain terrains tend to be rugged and, not infrequently, it becomes necessary to walk uphill to get somewhere. Much of the ground is covered with trees, all shapes and sizes—a bewildering experience for even the most methodical of dogs. In contrast, ocean beaches are reasonably flat, with soft, workable sand.

On the beaches one may observe dogs engaged in various digging operations. This is a neurotic habit adopted by many vacationing dogs, and studies show there are psychological reasons for their wanting to get underground:

1. To get away from people (escape mechanism).

2. To annoy other people on the beach (over-expression of hostility).

3. To build sleeping quarters (search for security).

4. To look for the shortest way to the place someone has just told them to go.

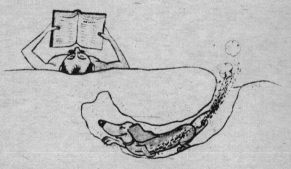

Almost anything the master decides to do on vacation is all right with the dog. In fact, no matter how silly the activity may seem, *the dog wants to go along to prove that there is no companion like the dog.*

Fishing appeals to the dog; he enjoys the excitement of waiting for the fish to bite, the war of nerves that precedes the catch.

Hunting trips offer an opportunity for the dog to prove his innate talents, the skills passed on to him by his ancestors.

Sightseeing is an activity dogs strongly approve of, especially if it is done as it should be: unhurriedly.

Mountain climbing may have its dangers, but its rewards are high. The fresh, invigorating air fills up one's lungs, gives tone to the muscles. The satisfaction of conquering the mountain "because it's there" makes the effort worthwhile.

|  | S M T W T F S |  |  | S M T W T F S |
|---|---|---|---|---|
| **JAN.** | (1)(2)<br>(3)(4)(5)(6)(7)(8)(9)<br>(10)(11)(12)(13)(14)(15)(16)<br>(17)(18)(19)(20)(21)(22)(23)<br>(24)(25)(26)(27)(28)(29)(30)<br>(31) | | **JULY** | (1)(2)<br>(3)(4)(5)(6)(7)(8)(9)<br>(10)(11)(12)(13)(14)(15)(16)<br>(17)(18)(19)(20)(21)(22)(23)<br>(24)(25)(26)(27)(28)(29)(30)<br>(31) |
| **FEB.** | (1)(2)(3)(4)(5)(6)<br>(7)(8)(9)(10)(11)(12)(13)<br>(14)(15)(16)(17)(18)(19)(20)<br>(21)(22)(23)(24)(25)(26)(27)<br>(28)(29) | | **AUG.** | (1)(2)(3)(4)(5)(6)<br>(7)(8)(9)(10)(11)(12)(13)<br>(14)(15)(16)(17)(18)(19)(20)<br>(21)(22)(23)(24)(25)(26)(27)<br>(28)(29)(30)(31) |
| **MAR.** | (1)(2)(3)(4)(5)<br>(6)(7)(8)(9)(10)(11)(12)<br>(13)(14)(15)(16)(17)(18)(19)<br>(20)(21)(22)(23)(24)(25)(26)<br>(27)(28)(29)(30)(31) | | **SEP.** | (1)(2)(3)<br>(4)(5)(6)(7)(8)(9)(10)<br>(11)(12)(13)(14)(15)(16)(17)<br>(18)(19)(20)(21)(22)(23)(24)<br>(25)(26)(27)(28)(29)(30) |
| **APR.** | (1)(2)<br>(3)(4)(5)(6)(7)(8)(9)<br>(10)(11)(12)(13)(14)(15)(16)<br>(17)(18)(19)(20)(21)(22)(23)<br>(24)(25)(26)(27)(28)(29)(30) | | **OCT.** | (1)<br>(2)(3)(4)(5)(6)(7)(8)<br>(9)(10)(11)(12)(13)(14)(15)<br>(16)(17)(18)(19)(20)(21)(22)<br>(23)(24)(25)(26)(27)(28)(29)<br>(30)(31) |
| **MAY** | (1)(2)(3)(4)(5)(6)(7)<br>(8)(9)(10)(11)(12)(13)(14)<br>15 16 (17)(18)(19)(20)(21)<br>(22)(23)(24)(25)(26)(27)(28)<br>(29)(30)(31) | | **NOV.** | (1)(2)(3)(4)(5)<br>(6)(7)(8)(9)(10)(11)(12)<br>(13)(14)(15)(16)(17)(18)(19)<br>(20)(21)(22)(23)(24)(25)(26)<br>(27)(28)(29)(30) |
| **JUNE** | (1)(2)(3)(4)<br>(5)(6)(7)(8)(9)(10)(11)<br>(12)(13)(14)(15)(16)(17)(18)<br>(19)(20)(21)(22)(23)(24)(25)<br>(26)(27)(28)(29)(30) | | **DEC.** | (1)(2)(3)<br>(4)(5)(6)(7)(8)(9)(10)<br>(11)(12)(13)(14)(15)(16)(17)<br>(18)(19)(20)(21)(22)(23)(24)<br>(25)(26)(27)(28)(29)(30)(31) |

When should your dog have his vacation? In the summer?
(It may be too hot for him.) In the winter? (It may be
too cold.) During the spring or fall? (These seasons may
be neither warm nor cool enough.)

Preferences of the average dog are shown here. Circles
around dates (O) show exactly when, in the dog's opinion, is the right time for vacationing.

94

# *Summary of Chapter 5*

1. DO take the dog with you on vacations. Remember: he, too, needs rest.

2. DON'T make him feel unwanted. Let him have the back seat of the car, if possible. If not possible, consider buying a new car.

3. DO choose your resorts carefully. The food served may make all the difference.

4. DON'T try to crowd too much into your vacation. Your dog is not used to it.

5. DO consider a trip to faraway places. It may inspire you to leave your dog there.

# 6

# Feeding the
# Neurotic Dog

Dog owners often complain that their dogs eat like pigs. Generally, there is no basis in fact for this accusation. Dogs do not eat like pigs. They eat like dogs.

The speed with which a dog can make food disappear is truly one of the wonders of nature. This is due to his capacity for swallowing food *in the whole,* no matter how large the portion. There has been some speculation as to why dogs do not chew; the answer is, of course, that chewing takes up valuable time.

Dogs eat for reasons of insecurity. They are afraid we might eat what belongs to them and, as a matter of fact, this notion is usually backed up by actual experience.

Sometimes dogs eat too much and become plump. Just when a dog is excessively overweight is not easily determined—he may merely be wholesome. As a rule, when your dog is no longer able to walk and has a tendency to roll over, it is time to cut down on his intake. Stop giving him food for several hours.

Overweight dogs can also be reduced by exercise. Some dogs naturally move about more than others. A lap dog must jump into and out of your lap several times a day; a watchdog, by contrast, lies still for long periods of time. Increasing the distance between his bed and his dish of food is one of the simple ways of giving your dog a more vigorous workout.

The best place to keep the dog's dish is in the kitchen. Next to the bedroom, this is the dog's favorite room. *It has been determined that a dog's concept of home is something like this:*

Simple, too, is the dog's idea of a kitchen.

Contrary to popular belief, the dog is not an omnivorous animal. He may accept an occasional egg, tomato, bowl of cereal, fruit salad, chopped chicken liver with radish garnish, grilled hickory ham and cheese on toast, or apple pie (either with cheese or à la mode), but, basically, he is carnivorous.

His ancestors stem from the wolf family *(Canis lupus)* and, consequently, dogs are meat eaters. Rugged instinct tells them to go for beef, veal, lamb, or pâté de foie gras.

A dog, however, will forego his natural preferences when he joins you at mealtimes. He has no affectations about table manners; he doesn't make a big fuss about what he eats as long as it is food. His technique for getting your attention while you are at your meal shows a well-developed sense of coordination.

Performance #1: Sitting-up exercises amuse people at table, even though they may have been doing that themselves for years. Reaction: "How cute." Food follows.

Performance #2: Special act is called for when dog is especially hungry.

Performance #3: Sitting in with the family and guests is the most practical solution.

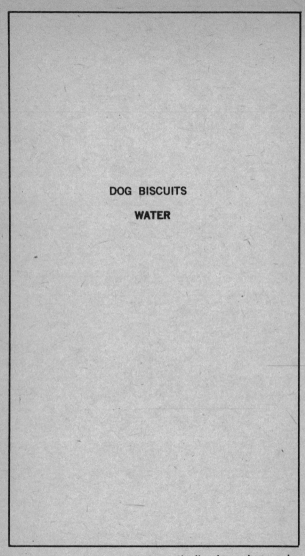

**DOG BISCUITS**

**WATER**

Man's idea of dog's meal dramatically shows human ig-
norance of canine needs.

# Menu

### ENTREES

Calf's Liver Steak Sauté, Smothered Onions, Mashed Potatoes
Filet of Veal Goulash à la Minute en Casserole, Rice
Calf's Sweetbreads Broiled, Potatoes Bouquetière
Hamburger Steak, Smothered Onions, Mashed Potatoes
Capon Cutlets, Creamed Mushrooms, Rissolé Potato
***Home-Made Bratwurst, Sauerkraut, Mashed Potatoes***
(2) Broiled Lamb Chops
Fresh Vegetable Dinner with Fried Egg
*Huhn im Topf (Boiled Chicken in Pot),*
  *Gemüse, Nudeln, Klösschen*
Chicken Fricassée with Rice; White Meat Only,
Fried Chicken à la Viennoise, Lettuce and Tomato, Rissolé Potato
***Sauerbraten und Kartoffel Klösse***
*Boiled Plate of Beef with Horseradish Sauce, Bouillon Potatoes
Jumbo Squab on Winekraut en Bordure or Jardinière
Fresh Chicken Livers Sauté with Apple Rings, Onions, Mashed
  Potatoes
(2) Pork Chops Broiled
Corned Pig's Knuckles, Sauerkraut, Mashed Potatoes

### FISH AND SEAFOOD

Filet of Sea Bass Sauté with Seedless Grapes, Boiled Potatoes
Boiled or Broiled Kennebec Salmon, Cucumber Salad
Broiled Pompano Maître d'Hôtel, Creamed Potatoes
Lobster Curried with Rice or à la Newburg, Chafing Dish
Broiled Swordfish, Potatoes Jardinière
Halibut Steak, Broiled, Parsley Potatoes
Frog's Legs Fried or Sauté Meunière, Mixed Salad
Fried Long Island Scallops, Tartar Sauce
Whole Imported English Sole Sauté Meunière, Mixed Salad
Creamed Crabflakes, Glazed Sherry Sauce
Fried Filet of Sole, Tartar Sauce, Potato Salad
State of Maine Lobster, Broiled

| CHEESE | FRUITS, COMPOTES |
|---|---|
| Imported Roquefort | Imported Bar-le-Duc |
| Welsh Rarebit | Baked Apple |
| Old Cheddar with Sherry | Melon in Season |
| Camembert | Apple Sauce. |
| Liederkranz | Half Grapefruit |
| Philadelphia Cream Cheese | *Importierte Preiselbeeren* |
| Pot Cheese | Fruit Cocktail |
| Bleu Cheese, Imported Type | Sliced Fruit in Season with |
| Canadian Okra | Cream |
| Imported Swiss Gruyère | Berries in Season with Cream |
| | Compote of Fruit |

Dog's idea of his menu points out major differences of
opinion between man and dog.

***You may want to put your dog on a diet.***
Few sights are as discouraging as a dog with a double chin. There are many reducing plans available, all of them analyzed for food value. The best-known are: Chef's Salad Diet, Water Diet, Gorge-Yourself-and-Be-Merry Diet, Two-Cucumbers-a-Day-for-the-Rest-of-Your-Life Diet, Breathe-While-You-Eat Diet, Eat-Nothing Diet, and Eat-Your-Way-to-the-Grave Diet. Choose the one that suits your dog's personality best.

Before you embark on your dog's feeding venture, however, you must decide just what it is you want from him. How much do you want him to lose? Half an ounce? Two ounces? Five ounces? or—if you happen to own a very large specimen (such as a St. Bernard or a Great Dane)—half a pound?

Reducing menus for dogs are simple to follow. Just keep in mind the caloric value of foods, the amount of vitamins in each item, the nutritional value, bacterial content, percentage of calcium, phosphorus, iron, and niacin. Don't forget the water content; over 90 per cent of one's body is nothing but water and the proportion becomes even greater with dogs about to be taken for a walk.

A few more pointers: Serve the dog boiled or poached eggs and avoid any fat in cooking them. Do not put cream in his coffee. Do not use sugar for sweetening; saccharin will do. Refrain from putting butter or margarine on his bread or on cooked vegetables.

***Dogs should not be disturbed while they eat.***
This rule is based not only on common courtesy but
also on the biological make-up of your dog. Thou-
sands of years ago the dog's forebears learned to protect their spoils against marauders, using all the
courage they could summon. This noble tradition is
carried on by the modern dog.

Special containers help dog maintain fast feeding speed. Such contrivances help him in his striving for canine fulfillment; they make him feel wanted.

Large chute funnels meal into dish, keeps food-level constant for several hours. Filling unit may be adjusted to dog's appetite.

Trough is highly recommended for its adaptability to well-rounded menu. Each compartment holds separate course. The widest one in the center is for the entrée.

Feeding bag is a useful supplement for dogs who eat while on the move.

# Summary of Chapter 6

1. DO feed your dog regularly; say, once an hour.

2. DON'T make him think he is an inferior member of your household. Let him join you at the table; this will go a long way toward making him feel *part of the family.*

3. DO keep in mind that dog food, as far as the dog is concerned, is for the birds, not for dogs. The dog was not consulted when man devised special foods for canines.

4. DON'T be misled by your dog's size. You may be larger than your dog, but you don't work as hard. He needs those calories.

# 7

# The Neurotic Dog
# vs. Baby

The greatest blow in the dog's life is the arrival of a baby in the family. The event puts extreme demands on the dog's already strained emotional life. It is easy to see why this is so.

**To the dog, the baby is just another dog— and not a very good one at that.** His head is way out of proportion to the rest of his body, his nose is too insignificant to have any practical value, his fur is visible only on the top of his head (if at all), his odor is not nearly as distinctive as that of most dogs. The human infant strikes a dog as a breed badly in need of some improvement.

Yet the master—judging from his actions—holds the new dog in as much, or perhaps greater, esteem than the present canine incumbent.

The new dog is fed not twice, but five or six times

a day. After he has consumed everything available, he is held, cuddled, spoken to in a soothing voice. His answers consist of belches—and this seems good enough for his audience.

He is not housebroken and shows no interest in learning, but this, too, is overlooked. When he bellows at night, he is not put out the back door as was the custom before he came; rather he is rocked to sleep with a lullaby. Should he make faces at his care-takers, they joyfully announce he is smiling at them, bless his little heart. His screams are referred to as healthy breathing exercises, his pulling of Mother's ears as outbursts of energy.

It soon becomes apparent to a dog that what's taking place shouldn't happen to a dog. Instinct tells him that . . .

# SOMEONE ELSE
## IS GETTING

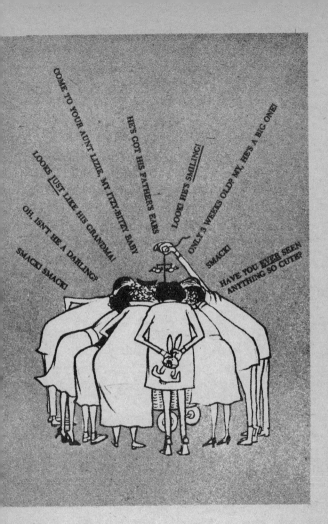

# ALL THE ATTENTION!

111

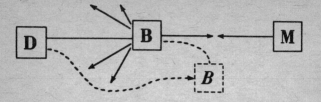

**Graphic demonstration** of dog's emotional dilemma after arrival of new baby. Dog (D) tries to get attention of Mother (M) by employing established habit patterns, such as walking up to her. Dog's route, however, is blocked by Baby (B), who has plans for himself. Dog tries to avoid physical violence by going around Baby, but Baby reacts with outward opposition (see dotted lines). Thus, conflict develops. Mother finally meets Baby halfway, ignoring dog, who leaves sulking (not shown in chart for lack of space).

Mother must learn early how to deal with sibling rivalry if she wants to raise a healthy family. There is no need to find a new home for the baby, if she approaches the problem with the proper psychological attitudes.

*The important thing to remember is that the dog was there first.* He has a right to be upset. Fortunately, parents can do much to help overcome the dog's feelings of resentment:

*1. Introduce the baby to the dog.* Try to explain to the dog that he is now going to have a little brother (or a little sister) whose diet will not interfere with that of the dog's in any way.

*2. Don't pet the baby in front of the dog.* If you must praise the baby, do it when the dog is out for a walk or busy in the kitchen.

**3. Don't forget your dog when you buy toys for the baby.** Always make sure there is an equal distribution of toys for each. This is one of the common-sense rules of parenthood.

**4. Scold the baby promptly if he bites the dog.** Tell him it isn't nice.

The slow physical development of the baby assures the dog of his superiority. As the months go by, the differences between the animal and the human become more pronounced; there can be no doubt about whose development is more rapid.

**2 MONTHS**

**4 MONTHS**

**6 MONTHS**

**8 MONTHS**

*Intellectual comparisons* also prove to the dog that he has it all over the infant. Baby develops slowly, if at all, and learns very little. In time, the dog leaves the human infant far behind in intellectual prowess, ability to reason, memory, and just plain common sense.

| BABY | DOG |
|---|---|
| **4 WEEKS** | **4 WEEKS** |
| He now breathes with regularity. He can cry. He opens his eyes wide. He can turn his head. | He now breathes with regularity. He can cry. He opens his eyes wide. He can turn his head. |
| **16 WEEKS** | **16 WEEKS** |
| He can turn over to his back. He can sit up (although he topples over). His eyes follow a moving object and he may even reach out for it. But he cannot grasp the object. | The puppy can walk across the room. He can sit, lie down, stand up. A moving object is followed by the eye and, if it is food, can be grasped quite well. |

| 28 WEEKS | 28 WEEKS |
|---|---|
| The baby can sit up, but he still tips over. He can reach for desired object and bring it to his mouth. He can even grab his feet and put them in his mouth as he lies on his back. | At this age, a puppy can do many things. He can get under blankets. He can chew hard cover books. He can bark, whine, howl, and emit a rich variety of sounds. He doesn't waste his time sucking his feet. |
| **1 YEAR** | **1 YEAR** |
| The baby creeps about freely on hands and knees. He is beginning to discover the world. | The dog can now run so fast only another dog can catch him. He has already discovered the world; he knows exactly where the kitchen and bedroom are located. |
| **2 YEARS** | **2 YEARS** |
| The baby now understands something of what is being said. He, himself, is able to utter a few words. In most cases, his toilet training is underway. | The dog understands everything that is being said (even understands that he must give the impression that he doesn't understand what is being said). He is housebroken and is puzzled about all the fuss that goes with teaching the baby what seems like a simple thing. |

Snuggling up while mother plays with the baby: Mother's attention can be captured by snuggling up close, butting head against her side.

Crying with the baby: Duet with screaming baby is a sure attention-getter that makes everyone in the house come running.

Rising to the situation, dogs size up their adversaries and take steps to ward off lasting effects of the intrusion. Realizing their position is now in serious jeopardy from someone who appears to have quite a calculating mind, dogs push themselves into the family limelight with truly remarkable persistence. Methods will vary, depending on the dog's ingenuity.

Participating at meals: Friendly participation at meals serves as a reminder that we **all** must eat in order to live.

Showing off skills: A demonstration of walking skill shows the parents which one is better at it.

The reader may surmise from this chapter that a baby and a dog are ardent enemies. This is not true. In time they learn to get along. The baby gets used to the dog's ways, even adopts some of them as his own. This pleases both the baby and the dog, if not the mother.

For example, there is the matter of toys. As far as the dog is concerned, his human friend's playthings fill a definite need. They are usually covered with non-toxic paint and are entirely harmless-tasting. Some of the gadgets (like metal spinning tops) are useless, to be sure, but most items are chewable and some can even be swallowed. As for the baby, he feels the same way about the dog's toys. They are meant for chewing, and a great many of them, if an effort is made, can be swallowed.

Most dogs will submit cheerfully to playing with babies. They will wrestle with the little one, tear his pants to pieces to the joy of both. They will play hide-and-go-seek in the living room, establishing meeting places under the couch where neither of them can be found. Let Mother call the baby for his meal, and they both will appear—the dog getting there a bit sooner. They will learn to share things. The dog will choose a few tidbits from the baby's dining table while the baby will be found at the dog's dish satisfying *his* appetite.

Soon, Mother will come to think of the dog as just another one of her children. This will not surprise the dog, since that is what he had in mind all along.

# Summary of Chapter 7

1. DON'T make your dog feel he comes second to the baby, especially if he came first.

2. DO consider that while a dog can be a playmate to a human infant, he can never be his intellectual companion. Humans are slow learners.

3. DON'T be surprised if your dog becomes strangely quiet and thoughtful for a few days after you bring your new baby home. He is figuring out ways to deal with the new situation.

4. DO tell your dog that he is not a natural child as soon as he is mature enough to understand he has been adopted.

# 8

# Analyzing the Neurotic Dog at Home

Psychoanalysis can be expensive, especially if both dog and master have to undergo treatment. Fortunately, the cost now can be cut in half. Today there are do-it-yourself methods for home analysis of pets.

Not much equipment is needed, just a soft couch on which he can lie, a hard chair on which you can sit. Tranquilizers may come in handy—if you are the excitable type.

Most dogs make cooperative patients. Lying on the couch for any length of time will put them in a quiet trance, a state commonly referred to as sleep. You will then have the opportunity to observe your patient and take notes.

Analysis is, of course, a slow, tedious process, and

---

results should not be expected overnight. The length of treatment may be 15 years, provided your dog lives that long. But, in the end, you will *understand* your dog.

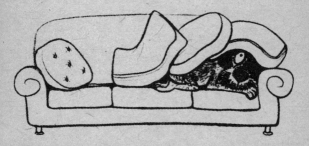

Pressing nose under arm of couch is a telltale sign of a basically shy, insecure individual. This type needs special treatment, a special couch for sure.

And, finally, a dog tired of living.

121

Quiet, darkened room will create the
right mood for the analysis to proceed.

## CANINE PERSONALITY QUIZ*

|  | Yes | No |
|---|---|---|
| 1. Does your dog like to watch television? | ( ) | ( ) |
| 2. Is he friendly when burglars enter the house? | ( ) | ( ) |
| 3. Does he join in community singing? | ( ) | ( ) |
| 4. Does he take long walks by himself? | ( ) | ( ) |
| 5. Does he jump in your lap the minute you sit down? | ( ) | ( ) |
| 6. Does he wrinkle his forehead when you talk to him? | ( ) | ( ) |
| 7. Does he seek out the sunny spots on your bed? | ( ) | ( ) |
| 8. Does he jump over the fence instead of using the gate? | ( ) | ( ) |
| 9. Does he sniff at his food before tasting it? | ( ) | ( ) |
| 10. Does he like to sleep inside your closet? | ( ) | ( ) |

Score plus 5 for each affirmative answer to questions 1, 4, 6, 9, 10, 12, 13. Score minus 5 for each affirmative answer to questions 2, 3, 5, 7, 8, 11, 14. If you have a plus answer, your dog is basically an introvert; if you have a minus answer, your dog is basically an extrovert.

You are neither an introvert nor an extrovert if you didn't mark any of the questions. You're just not paying attention.

11. Does he spend a great deal of time chasing flies, birds, and rabbits he cannot ever hope to catch?    ( )   ( )

12. Does he drink a lot?    ( )   ( )

13. Does he spend much time looking out the window, brooding about the traffic, women's hats, where the next meal is coming from?    ( )   ( )

14. Does he smile often?    ( )   ( )

*Here is how these conclusions to the quiz have been arrived at:*

1. If your dog likes to watch television, he is escaping from reality. He is an introvert.

2. If your dog welcomes burglars, he must be the social type. He is an extrovert.

3. Singing is a group activity. He sings, he feels part of the crowd. He is an extrovert.

4. Only lone wolves take solitary walks. Your dog is a lone wolf. He is an introvert.

5. He likes you. He is an extrovert.

6. Anxiety complex makes dog scowl. He is an introvert.

7. Happy dogs will seek out the sunny spot on the bed. They will fight for it. He is an extrovert.

8. A contented dog will leap high whenever possible. He will prefer to jump over your fence even if he doesn't quite make it. He is an extrovert.

9. A dog with a suspicious nature will sniff at food before tasting it. He is an introvert.

10. Dark corners inside closets beckon the personality who wishes to withdraw from the world. He is an introvert.

11. Chasing flies may not make much sense, but why not? He is an extrovert.

12. Drinking is just another way to escape from reality. He is an introvert.

13. He is an observer but not a participator. He is an introvert.

14. A dog with a quick smile is a cheerful dog. Smile back at him. He is an extrovert. Introverts do not smile.

Outer surface of dog's skull tells much about brain beneath, if any. Different breeds display different shapes of heads, i.e., egg-head, pumpkin-head, square-head; and the inverted-pyramid head. Regardless of outside appearance, all heads are made up of component parts. The upper part joins with the lower part, the front part with the back part—a tidy arrangement provided by nature.

Of great significance, according to canine phrenologists, are the bumps on a dog's head. Nasal bones end in a knob (1), called nose in scientific circles, schnozzle by the average dog-lover. This bump serves as an olfactory device, helpful to the intellectually curious who want to know where they can find the food.

Prominent dome-like protuberance at top of head is an important skull formation (2) since it serves as forehead, starting place for ears, eyes, and (usually) clump of hair (3).

Slight rise on back of dog's head (4) is only a so-called "temporary bump," put there by another dog or, possibly, by a kick in the head.

**Facial expressions of sleeping dog**
allow observer to delve into the sub-
conscious for hidden feelings of the

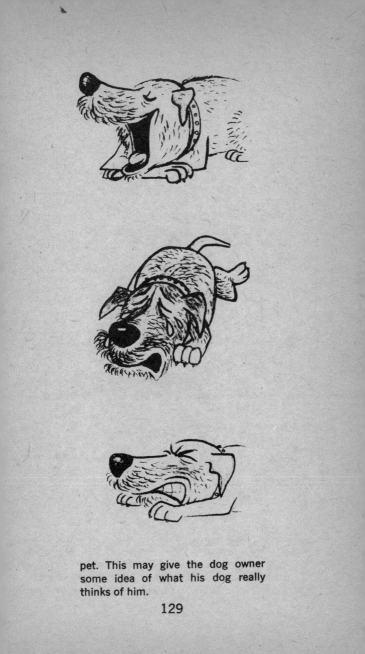

pet. This may give the dog owner some idea of what his dog really thinks of him.

**Maze tests** are commonly used in laboratories to check intelligence of animals. You can now set up such a test in your own home. All you need is a dish of food and a dog. The rest will take care of itself.

130

If you can, try to count in your mind the seconds it takes the dog to reach the source of food. The results will enable you to estimate accurately the Reasoning Power of your dog (R/P), his Personality Quotient (P/Q), and his ability to run (A/R).

**Alertness Test** (to test your dog's alertness) is a simple procedure. Call him by name. Watch his reaction closely. To make sure you are giving him every opportunity to react to your efforts, repeat his name

Average dog will react when he hears his name called the third time. Tolerant by nature, he will listen to what you have to say before going back to sleep.

Exceptionally alert dog will probably open his eyes the second time his name is mentioned, and keep them that way a little longer. He may even give you a fleeting smirk, showing his good will toward all men, including you.

Relaxed dog knows better (he's probably seen this test administered before). Since his eyes remain closed, there is no real way of checking his reaction to your unrestrained screaming.

four or five times, raising your voice each time. Toward the completion of the test, scream as loud as you can. Take notes so you can compare them with the types shown here.

**Sociability Test** will enable you to measure your dog's interest in his fellow dogs. Healthy, well-adjusted dogs

will greet one another, exchange views, and then be on their way to make, somewhere else, another new friend.

# ANY OTHER SYMPTOMS?

Watch for them . . .

NOW . . . **AT LAST** . . . YOU UNDERSTAND
YOUR DOG

# *Summary of Chapter 8*

1. DO psychoanalyze your dog. It will help him to face himself, and even more important, it will help you to face him.

2. DON'T waste your money on professional fees for your dog's analysis. You will need that money to pay for your own treatments.

3. DO get to know your dog. You may be surprised at the things you find out about him.

4. DON'T hurry with the analysis. Remember: your dog likes to lie on the couch.

5. DO keep your dog.

# 9
# Can the Neurotic Dog Be Cured?

No.